Paines Plough, Live T
and Ellie Keel Pro(
Synergy Th(

ORDINARY DECENT CRIMINAL

BY ED EDWARDS

Ordinary Decent Criminal was first performed at Live Theatre, Newcastle, on 23 July 2025, before a tour of the UK including Summerhall at the Edinburgh Festival Fringe from 31 July 2025.

ORDINARY DECENT CRIMINAL

BY ED EDWARDS

Performer	Mark Thomas
Writer	Ed Edwards
Director	Charlotte Bennett
Set & Costume Designer	Lydia Denno
Sound Designer	Elena Peña
Lighting Designer	Drummond Orr
Dramaturg	Neil Grutchfield
Sound Associate	Raffaela Pancucci
Voice & Dialect Coach	Emma Woodvine
Company Stage Manager	Tine Selby

Mark Thomas | Performer

Mark Thomas is a comic, theatremaker and writer... Oh, and now actor.

He has won five Fringe First awards, a Herald Angel award, an Amnesty International Freedom of Expression Award, a Stage Special Contribution Award, The Howard Street Theatre Award, a Lustrum Award, a Time Out Award for contribution to comedy, a MISTY media activist award, a UN Association Global Human Rights Defender Award, the Kurdish Congress Medal of Honour and a Sony Radio Award. He was awarded an Honorary Doctorate and is a Doctor of Letters from Bradford Uni and in 2022 was awarded an Honorary Doctorate and is a Doctor of Arts from Kent University. He appeared on three series of *The Mary Whitehouse Experience* radio show on Radio 1, Hosted *Loose Talk* topical comedy show on Radio 1 for three series and ran his own show *The Manifesto* show for three series on Radio 4.

TV show *The Mark Thomas Comedy Product* ran for six series on Channel 4, during which the show cost more than one MP their career, exposed corruption in Department of Trade and Industry deals, put an arms dealer in jail, changed tax law in the UK and arms control in Europe; and bet an entire shows budget on a horse. He has written six books and had four playscripts published. Mark has performed his shows at the National Theatre on three occasions. He walked the entire length of the Israeli wall, wrote and performed about the experience.

Mark set up a comedy club in a refugee camp on Jenin in the West Bank, a project that is still running and aims to create a comedy circuit in Palestine. He wrote and performed a play about the Palestinian club which toured the UK featuring two Palestinian performers, Faisal and Alaa.

He has curated two art exhibitions, one of which appeared in Venezuela. He has given evidence before Parliamentary Select Committees on three occasions. He has taken the police to court four times, won three, the fourth is pending in Europe. He's also won compensation from the Met – twice – for wrongful stop-and-search and curtailing the right to protest. He was spied upon by BAE Systems which was proven in court, and he wrote an award-winning show about it. He won ten thousand pounds of compensation from the Construction Blacklist companies including Skanska, Balfour Beatty, McAlpine and Taylor Woodrow. He held the world record for most political demonstrations in a day and has a Guinness Book of World Records certificate to prove it! He helped unionise the Curzon cinema chain. He was a columnist at the New Statesman for four years. He ran the Ilisu Dam Campaign for three years targeting dam building in the Kurdish region of Turkey. He took UK government to court twice, once over the Iraq war and once when serious fraud office collapsed the investigation into bribery between Saudi Arabia and BAE systems. The later case resulted in a victory only to be overturned by the Supreme Court.

He has three children.

Ed Edwards | Writer

Ed Edwards is an ex-offender and multi-award-winning playwright. Ed wrote his first novel while awaiting trial on drugs charges. The novel was published the day he was sentenced to three-and-a half-years in jail, so his second novel (published by Fourth Estate) was written inside. Clean and sober ever since, Ed went on to write for *Brookside*, *The Bill* and *Holby City* and write original plays for BBC Radio 4.

Ed currently teaches part-time at the University of Greater Manchester and writes for theatre. Ed's play *The Political History of Smack and Crack* was a finalist at the Theatre503 Playwriting competition, appearing at Paines Plough's Roundabout at Edinburgh Fringe, and went on to tour nationally. His last play, *England & Son* – written specifically for the comedian and activist Mark Thomas – also performed at Roundabout and won multiple awards, including a Fringe First and an Offie, then transferred to Adelaide Theatre festival where it also won a Best Theatre award.

Ed is currently Writer on attachment at the National Theatre.

Charlotte Bennett | Director

Charlotte Bennett joined Paines Plough as Joint Artistic Director alongside Katie Posner in August 2019. For Paines Plough, Charlotte has directed *My Mother's Funeral: The Show* by Kelly Jones (Fringe First winner 2024); *Reasons You Should(n't) Love Me* by Amy Trigg (winner of the Women's Prize for Playwriting) which premiered at Kiln Theatre in May 2021 before embarking upon a UK tour of seventeen venues and returning to the Kiln in November 2022; and *Run Sister Run* by Chloë Moss (Sheffield Theatres/Soho Theatre).

Previously she was Associate Director at Soho Theatre where she led the new writing department, developing artists and commissions and programming. For Soho Theatre, she directed *Whitewash* by Gabriel Bisset-Smith, *Happy Hour* by Jack Rooke, curated a six-month off-site arts festival in Waltham Forest and led playwriting competition the Verity Bargate Award. Prior to this she was Artistic Director of Forward Theatre Project; an artists' collective she founded. For Forward Theatre Project she made and directed new plays which toured nationally inspired by working in partnership with different communities around the UK and at venues including the National Theatre, York Theatre Royal, Northern Stage, Derby Theatre, Live Theatre and The Lowry.

As a freelance director she has worked extensively for Open Clasp Theatre Company creating new plays inspired by women in the North-East and she held the role of Producer for theatre company RashDash for four years where she toured experimental new theatre around the UK.

Lydia Denno | Set & Costume Designer

Lydia is an interdisciplinary artist whose practice encompasses theatre, installation, illustration and even walking. She has worked extensively for regional and London theatres, as well as heritage sites and galleries internationally. She is drawn towards under-represented stories and characters, is inspired by what can be communicated in visual fragments and fleeting moments, and excited by the stories that lie in the detail.

Elena Peña | Sound Designer

For Paines Plough: *Reasons You Should(n't) Love Me* by Amy Trigg (Kiln Theatre & UK tour). Recent theatre includes: *The Beautiful Future Is Coming* (Bristol Old Vic); *Rhinoceros* (Almeida); *A Good House* (Bristol Old Vic/ Royal Court); *The Legends of Them* (Royal Court/ Hackney Showroom/ Brixton House); *A Tupperware of Ashes*,*The Hot Wing King* (National Theatre); *The Wedding Band* (Lyric Hammersmith); *Sweat* (Royal Exchange); *Liberation Squares* (Nottingham Playhouse); *Blue Mist**, *Baghdaddy*, *two palestinians go dogging** (Royal Court); *Cinderella* (Brixton House); *As You Like It* (RSC) *Olivier Award nominations for Outstanding Achievement in Affiliate Theatre. Film Includes: *Hope* (Clean Break); *The Magic Finger* (Unicorn). Radio/ Podcast includes: *Rockpool*; *The Meet Cute*; *Twelve Years*. Dance includes: *Patrias*; *Quimeras*.

Drummond Orr | Lighting Designer

Drummond has over 40 years experience as a theatre electrician, technical manager, lighting designer and production manager. In that time, he has toured nationally and internationally. Lighting design credits include: *Cooking with Elvis*, *Motherland*, *The Prize*, *Captain Amazing* (Live Theatre/ Edinburgh Fringe); *Cilla and Me*, *Iris*, *My Romantic History*, *Tyne*, *Nativities*, *The Savage*, *Harriet Martineau Dreams of Dancing*, *The Cold Buffet*, *Three Acts of Love*, *Saint Maud*, *Champion*, *Dogs on the Metro* (Live Theatre); *The Bounds* (Live Theatre/ Royal Court); *The Red Lion* (Live Theatre/Trafalgar Studios); *Wet House* (Live Theatre/Hull Truck/Soho Theatre); *A Walk On Part* (LiveTheatre/Soho Theatre/ Arts Theatre); *The Girl in the Yellow Dress* (Market Theatre, Johannesburg/ Grahamstown Festival/Baxter Theatre, Cape Town/Citizens, Glasgow); *Educating Rita* (Theatre by the Lake/David Pugh and UK Tour).

Neil Grutchfield | Dramaturg

Neil is the New Writing Manager at Synergy Theatre Project where he has 15 years' experience working with prisoner and ex-prisoner playwrights, as well as professional writers writing about criminal justice. A freelance dramaturg for over 20 years, Neil has worked with emerging, mid-career and senior playwrights. In 2021 he was shortlisted for the Kenneth Tynan Award for dramaturgy. Theatre includes: *The Boy* by Joakim Daun (Soho); *Vessel* by Laura Wyatt O'Keefe (tour); *Pot* by Ambreen Razia (Oval House/Stratford Circus). For Synergy Theatre Project: *The Special Relationship* by Hassan Abdulrazzak (Soho); *There Is A Field* by Martin Askew (Theatre503).

Raffaela Pancucci | Sound Associate

Training: Theatre Sound at The Royal Central School of Speech and Drama. As Sound Designer: *1:17am* (Theatre503); *Marshmallow Me* (Harlow Playhouse, Red Lion Theatre); *Basic Bald B*tch* (Brixton House); *Last Black Girl on Earth* (Camden Roundhouse); *Invisible Animal*, *Phaedra* (Omnibus); *Then, Now & Next* (Southwark Playhouse Borough); *Beasts* (ZOO Playground Edinburgh); *Choose Your Fighter* (Camden People's Theatre); *Please Feel Free to Share* (Pleasance Edinburgh, Theatre503). As Associate Sound Designer: *Figures in Extinction* (European Tour); *War Horse* (UK tour); *Death of England Trilogy* (@sohoplace); *Death of England: Closing Time* (Dorfman Theatre); *Stranger Things: The First Shadow* (as Workshop Assistant).

Emma Woodvine | Voice & Dialect Coach

Theatre includes: *The Government Inspector* (Chichester); *Abigail's Party*, *Gypsy* (Royal Exchange Manchester); *Hamlet*, *Cymbeline*, *Imperium* (RSC); *Ghosts*, *Julius Caesar*, *As You Like it*, *The Tempest*, *Swive* (Shakespeare's Globe); *Word-Play*, *Hang*, *Routes* (Royal Court); *Fun Home*, *The Scottsboro Boys*, *Wings*, *Happy Days*, *Galileo* (Young Vic); *The Trials* (Donmar); *Machinal* (Almeida); *King Lear*, *My Neighbour Totoro*, *Ghost the Musical* (West End); *Beautiful: the Carole King Musical*, *Fisherman's Friends* (UK tour); *Love Life*, *Street Scene*, *Kiss Me Kate*, *Carousel* (Opera North). Film includes: *Mayday*, *Rose of Nevada*, *Widow Clicquot*, *Black Mirror: Demon79*, *Cyrano*, *Darkest Hour*. Television includes: *Tiny Tunes*, *Christopher and His Kind*.

Tine Selby | Company Stage Manager

Since graduating from the Guildhall School of Music and Drama in 1987, Tine has stage managed indoor and outdoor theatre and put power and lights into festivals all around the UK. A former operations manager at South Street Arts Centre in Reading, Tine is also an experienced technical manager and production stage manager. In 2012 she settled down to the more relaxing (!) world of tour management and production, working on national and international tours for Ruby Wax and Mark Thomas.

Hello! We're Paines Plough. We're a theatre company that specialises in new writing, led by Joint Artistic Directors Charlotte Bennett and Katie Posner. As a touring company dedicated to new writing, we discover, develop and empower writers and share their explosive new stories with audiences all over the UK and beyond.

Founded in 1974, we have worked with over 500 playwrights including Sarah Kane, Abi Morgan, Dennis Kelly, Miriam Battye, James Graham, Nathan Bryon, Kae Tempest, Vinay Patel, Mike Bartlett, Chloë Moss and Anna Jordan.

Our plays are nationally discovered and locally heard. Each year, we tour our shows to over 30,000 people and work with 400 writers through our nationwide, multi-year writer development programme, Tour The Writer.

In 2019, alongside Ellie Keel, we co-founded the Women's Prize for Playwriting to redress the imbalance of stories being told on our national stages, and we have co-produced and toured three of the winners so far: *Reasons You Should(n't) Love Me* by Amy Trigg, *You Bury Me* by Ahlam, and *Consumed* by Karis Kelly.

Joint Artistic Directors & CEOs	Charlotte Bennett & Katie Posner
Executive Director (Incoming)	Claire Simpson
Interim Executive Director	Lilli Geissendorfer
Senior Producer	Ellie Fitz-Gerald
Marketing and Audience Development Manager	Manwah Siu
Administrator	Hannah Churchill
Press Representative	Bread and Butter PR

'An essential part of the UK's new writing ecology.'
Lyn Gardner, *Stage Door*

Board of Directors
Ankur Bahl, Corey Campbell, Lauren Dark, Asma Hussain, Helen Perryer, Farha Quadri, Carolyn Saunders, Kully Thiarai (Chair).

office@painesplough.com
painesplough.com

Donate to Paines Plough at **justgiving.com/PainesPlough**

Paines Plough Limited is a company limited by guarantee and a registered charity.
Registered Company no: 1165130. Registered Charity no: 267523
Paines Plough Offices, Belgrade Theatre, Belgrade Square, Corporation St, Coventry, CV1 1GS

'One of the most fertile crucibles of new writing'
Guardian

Our vision is for a North East that writes its own story and fights for a more creative future.

Live Theatre occupies a unique place as one of the country's only dedicated new writing buildings outside of London. For over fifty years it has launched the careers of many of today's leading theatre figures and continues to develop and platform the artists of tomorrow, from playwrights to local school children. Deeply connected to its region and unafraid to confront the most pressing issues of our time, Live Theatre brings ambitious regional artists and adventurous local audiences into vivid contact.

Our mission is to unearth the rich and unexpected narratives of our region, to nurture creativity and bring passionate ideas to life and to be a space that unites people and ignites imaginations.

'Live Theatre has supported generation after generation of new writers, actors and theatre artists.'
Lee Hall, Playwright

Artistic Director/Joint Chief Executive   Jack McNamara
Executive Director/Joint Chief Executive   Jacqui Kell
New Work Producer   JD Stewart

To learn more about Live Theatre and get involved, go to **live.org.uk**

Theatre Royal Plymouth (TRP) is a registered charity and the largest regional producing theatre in the UK housing three theatres – The Lyric, The Drum and The Lab. TR2, Theatre Royal's Production and Learning Centre, is an award-winning production house that combines internationally regarded scenic design and construction projects with state-of-the-art rehearsal studios.

TRP provides art, education and community engagement in Plymouth and across the region to 30,000 people per year, aiming to strengthen the creative community in Plymouth and surrounding areas. The theatre maintains an annual audience of 300,000 people and presents a year-round programme of world class productions on all scales as the South West's principal centre for performing arts.

Recent TRP co-productions include *The Artist* (with The McOnie Company & Playful Productions) *The Devil Wears Prada* (with Kevin McCollum/Alchemation, Rocket Entertainment/David Furnish and Jamie Wilson) and *The Creakers* (with Smith & Brant & Impossible Producing)

TRP Executive Team
Chief Executive and Artistic Director   James Mackenzie-Blackman
Deputy CEO, Finance and Operations   Helen Costello
Deputy CEO, Producing and Programming   Liz King

theatreroyal.com

EKP

Winner: The Stage Producer of the Year 2024

Founded in 2019, Ellie Keel Productions commissions, develops and produces fearlessly imaginative new plays. Recent work includes the Olivier Award-nominated *The Swell* by Isley Lynn (Orange Tree Theatre, 2023) and *Bullring Techno Makeout Jamz* by Nathan Queeley-Dennis (Paines Plough Roundabout & Royal Court Theatre, both 2023; UK tour, 2024).

Other recent productions include the critically-acclaimed and award-winning shows *An Interrogation* by Jamie Armitage (Summerhall, Edinburgh, 2023; Hampstead Theatre, 2025), *Bellringers* by Daisy Hall (Paines Plough Roundabout, 2024; Hampstead Theatre, 2024), *The Last Show Before We Die* by Mary Higgins and Ell Potter (Paines Plough Roundabout, 2023), *You Bury Me* by Ahlam (Bristol Old Vic, Royal Lyceum Theatre & Orange Tree Theatre, 2023), and *Sap* by Rafaella Marcus (Paines Plough Roundabout, 2022; Soho Theatre & UK tour, 2023).

Other notable EKP shows include *Reasons You Should(n't) Love Me* by Amy Trigg (Kiln Theatre, 2021; UK tour, 2022), *Collapsible* by Margaret Perry (HighTide Festival at Assembly; Dublin's Abbey Theatre, 2019; Bush Theatre, 2020), *Hotter* by Mary Higgins and Ell Potter (Underbelly, 2019l Soho Theatre and tour), *Still No Idea* by Lisa Hammond and Rachael Spence (Traverse Theatre, Southbank Centre & UK tour, 2019), and *Fitter* by Mary Higgins and Ell Potter (Soho Theatre, 2019-20).

Ellie Keel Productions are co-founders of the Women's Prize for Playwriting.

Executive Producer   Ellie Keel
Producer   Natasha Ketel

synergy theatre project

Synergy Theatre Project creates ground-breaking work which harnesses the energy, creativity and life experiences of those we work with – prisoners, ex-prisoners, young offenders and young people at risk of offending. We give them a voice and, in doing so, their dignity back. We inspire change by affecting feelings, attitudes and behaviour, and provide practical opportunities which build a bridge from prison to social reintegration.

We are also concerned with the impact of our work on the public and use stories to humanise and provide new insights into the criminal justice system. Central to our approach is a commitment to artistic quality and empowerment of participants with the work taking place both in theatres, prisons and non-traditional venues. We play to diverse audiences and promote mutual exchange between performers and audiences to break down social barriers.

Staff

Artistic Director	Esther Baker
General Manager	Jennie McClure
New Writing Manager	Neil Grutchfield
Learning & Engagement Manager	Kit Withington
Learning & Engagement Manager (Young people)	Siân Henderson
Learning & Engagement Coordinator (Young people)	Shane Wheeler-Osman
Learning & Engagement Assistant	Karl Smith
Marketing Manager	Vic Shead

Board of Trustees
Keshina Bouri
Paula Hamilton
Tyrone Paul
Ihsan Rahim
Clióna Roberts
Gaby Sumner

Patron
Martin McDonagh

synergytheatreproject.co.uk
@synergytheatreproject

ORDINARY DECENT CRIMINAL

Ed Edwards

Notes on the Text

Direct address in plain text.

Dialogue and thoughts in italics.

(*Occasional stage directions or clarifications in brackets.*)

Lines can be taken as stage directions as seen fit.

This text went to press before the end of rehearsals and so may differ slightly from the play as performed.

1.

Picture Ancient Rome. In the early nineteen-nineties. Somewhere between Liverpool and Manchester.

Proletarians gather on the landings, overlooking. Unsure what to expect.

But something's coming, you can feel it.

No screw anywhere in sight. Just us. The multitude.

A wiry-looking con struts through the door at the end of the ones. Shouts,

Levins is a grass!

The words echo. There's a hush.

This is it now.

A gaunt man enters. Unaware.

Again the call. *Levins is a <u>grass</u>!*

Christian sees Lion – and us.

Levins trudges into the bathroom followed by the Lion.

There's bangs and screams. For a long time.

The Accuser comes out unscathed, gets off sharpish.

Levins stumbles out, bloodied. Looks about. Defiant finally.

I'm not a fucking grass!

Goes to get his ear sewn back on.

2.

(*Smokes.*) The first time I get stoned as a lad in South London I lie there thinking,

Wow – now I can actually fucking live!

My mate Jonno gets stabbed outside his uncle's boxing gym in a stupid fight over nothing – my world turns to shit – nothing makes sense – I hate everything – something has to change – fuck knows what – what can I do? – but suddenly – (*Smokes.*) the world's still shit – Jonno's still in his wheelchair – but – me? – I feel good.

I feel fantastic!

I use drugs every day from that moment on to stay sane.

So. It's only logical: when I finally stop using – in the early nineteen-nineties – aged thirty – I'm insane again.

Example.

When I get clean – and this is total abstinence – I carry on dealing.

I'm importing half-kilos of cannabis resin – through the post – from Spain – disguised as chocolate bars. Seriously.

I share about it in my Narcotics Anonymous meetings. Because, well, meetings are all about getting real, yeah?

After the Friday meeting Little Phil sidles up to me and says,

…He's dead nice, Phil…

I'm not judging you, Frankie, but. You might find dealing drugs will interfere with your recovery.

I'm like, *Yeah, yeah, I know. I'm gonna stop. I'm gonna stop.*

Phil nods, sagely.

But it's harder to stop dealing than you think.

It's the buzz.

And the rolls of cash.

And you know, there's things to pay for. But we'll get to Josie.

Don't tell her I said that!

It's a lot easier to stop dealing when *Customs and Excise* turn up on your doorstep.

*

I get back to my place in Manchester one night and there's two men with moustaches waiting for me.

Never a good sign.

As I get out of my car Big Moustache says,

Are you Frankie Donnelly?

I deny it strenuously.

Little Moustache flashes an ID and says,

That's funny, cos we were told a man answering your description with a London accent lives here. Can we come in and talk to you?

Now, I have got some experience dealing with the law. From my political activist days.

So I say – (*Dublin accent.*) *Have either of you wee fellas gorra warrant?*

This is the moment I discover it's different being arrested for a real crime – as opposed to say, chaining yourself to the underside of a bus full of arms dealers.

No one chanting your name outside the nick this time.

Or cheering when you get out.

Anyhow. Long story short. After a year on bail. Still clean and sober. I'm sentenced to three-and-a-half years for importation. Which…

As Norman – who I sell with – always says, *Can you imagine Frankie in jail?!*

They all fall about laughing.

And I laugh too. Because... Let's just say I lack a right hook.

It's a matter of principle, actually. I mean my mate Jonno, who got stabbed, had a top right hook and look where that got him.

Bit of luck, though. Shortly before I'm sentenced they burn HMP Strangeways to the ground.

Which means the fascist bastard who runs Strangeways before the uprising wants to prove he's not a fascist bastard when he's appointed Governor of his next jail. Where I end up.

So it's kind of more *New Labour* than Margaret Thatcher.

(*Showing us round.*) You get a cell to yourself. Unheard of now.

Sink. Proper toilet. Should've packed one of them fluffy covers.

Oh, and there's phones if you can hustle a prison phone card.

I should point out though...

Just because it's not your pre-uprising Strangeways hellhole – it doesn't mean I'm not still...

Fucking terrified!

3.

Kenny's in bed at home in Salford.

He's a good lad when you get to know him.

He's got these cool-looking sheets hanging up in his bedroom. Across the ceiling and round the walls.

Coloured material he nicked from school a few years ago. Calico, it's called.

String of coloured lights over the top. Looks mint.

Some of the bulbs have gone, but.

He doesn't want people to see it, though. Kenny doesn't like people coming in his room.

Hates it, in fact.

He's listening to Nico and The Velvets.

He's got a thing about The Velvets and John Cale and Iggy Pop and none of his old schoolmates have even heard of them.

Which he loves.

There's a creak on the floorboards outside. By the bathroom.

He tenses up. Feels that sliding, inside.

His mum's on nights again.

But her boyfriend's in.

Pete's footsteps stop outside his room.

Kenny holds his breath. But no…

Footsteps creak away.

Relief.

Mixed with disappointment.

He's waited all day for this!

His mum's bedroom door clicks shut. Pete's gone to bed.

Kenny lies there thinking about Pete.

For once, really thinking about him.

The bastard!

He feels sick. Grips the knife under the covers.

Pushes it into his thigh near the top. Grits his teeth.

Aagh!

Drop of blood. More than a drop.

Nice.

Then,

Decision.

He's up.

Moving.

Doorhandle.

Light on the landing's <u>nasty</u>!

Keep going.

He falls into his mum's bedroom.

Flash of Pete in a shaft of light from the door.

Shouting.

Kenny doesn't remember stabbing Pete twenty-seven times.

He's surprised to hear it later.

He remembers Pete jumping over him, though.

Like, six foot in the air.

Jumps right over him. Runs onto the street. Falls over in the road.

Kenny goes back to his room.

Gets into bed.

Squints at the stars in the calico.

4.

A few nights in, I make my first Big Mistake.

It's all about my book.

(*Explaining.*) When I'm out on bail I write a novel which actually gets published.

It's only a punk publishers. Which is a thing in the nineties. This posh guy I sell to runs it.

You should write about dealing and being a fuck-up, Frankie. I mean, 'Write What You Know', eh. Ha ha.

We sell three-hundred-and-sixteen copies and get a review in the *Yorkshire Post*. So big time, yeah?

Seriously, I've always written. It got me respect round our way. Made up for the lack of a right hook.

Anyhow. I already feel like a pig at a wedding in here so I decide. *Tell No One about the book.*

No one.

But then there's the White Muslim.

Most people only say they're Muslim to get on the Muslim diet – which is brought in from outside and looks amazing.

But this guy takes it seriously.

He's not big but I find out later he's running the entire nick.

He comes over just before bang-up and says, *It's your first time, innit.*

I say, *Does it show?*

He asks what I'm in for and when I tell him he says, *Suicide mission was it?*

I indignantly explain how the cannabis bars are dipped in wax before the chocolate so the sniffer dogs can't detect it. Professional-like.

He shakes his head like a disappointed father. Says,

I do it properly, me. You need a proper business. Importing carpets. Or fruit. Bring stuff in with it that's actually worth something...

Meaning heroin.

(*Still the White Muslim.*) ...*This is my first sentence in thirty years. Expensive brief – defended Ronnie Biggs – got it down to six. It's a rest for me, this. Last time I was here I was fifteen years old. Same screw – still on reception – recognises me.*

(*Impression of the screw.*) *Hey, I know you. You haven't changed, then!*

(*Back to the White Muslim.*) *I look him dead in the eye and say: I've got a condo in Florida – house in Southport – beautiful wife – lovely girlfriend – kids in private school. I've travelled the world and you're still in this nasty nick, doing the same nasty job? Who's doing the life sentence, eh? ...You should've seen his face, the twat.*

I'm laughing now. Until he looks <u>me</u> dead in the eye and says,

You don't seem the type to be importing.

Which is him saying, *Are you a nonce?*

Which if I am: death sentence.

I say, *Actually I'm a writer. I've just written a book. That's it there, look.*

His face changes. Like magic.

He says he loves reading. That he's reading the Qur'an. In a special translation. That brings out the language and makes the hair on the back of his arms stand on end.

Then he says,

Can I read your book?

I say, *Of course!*

He shakes my hand and says he's called Robert – as in DeNiro – which is what people call him.

As I hand DeNiro my book, I remember the gay sex scene.

5.

An hour after bang-up I'm still pacing.

I mean. It's just a gay sex scene.

A fictional character – <u>fictionally</u> – has sex with a guy he's been mates with forever – the tough one – who surprisingly comes out of the closet – no one expected that! – and now you look he's actually – well – quite cute. And the <u>me</u> character – who <u>isn't</u> me – finds it surprisingly nice. Even though he's straight. Which is made <u>very clear</u> in the book.

It's near the end. He might not get that far.

What was it Kieran from back home wrote me when he heard I'd been busted?

Yo dickhead! They'll have you tottering down the landing in a bin-liner skirt!

I look terrible in a skirt because of my housemaid's knee. Sticks right out when it flares up.

I'm gonna talk about Josie. A lot.

Macho man! (*Pose.*)

Ouch. (*His knee hurts.*)

6.

Dear Frankie,

A couple of days later I get my first beautiful letter from Josie.

And I am right back with you…

*

(*Reliving his experience.*) I come back to the house and you're out the back, in the sun, naked.

I'm stunned. I've wanted you for so long, but…? Not like this.

You sit up. Pleased to see me. Shade your eyes from the sun.

I'm shocked how thin you've got.

You say, *Was he in?*

I nod and hand you a bag of heroin I've scored for you.

I keep the other bag in my pocket.

You know it's there, but we don't saying anything about it.

You jump up and stride into the house. *Thanks, Frankie.*

*

I pick Jay-Jay up from school.

Your gorgeous little boy.

I make pasta and pesto and broccoli with hummus for us all while Jay-Jay watches telly.

You don't eat much. But you do have three of Jay-Jay's lunchbox Frubes for your pudding.

I always buy extras.

Jay-Jay talks about the *Teenage Mutant Ninja Turtle*s – and his eyes shine with the thoughts of it.

*

Later I go out with my massive mobile phone on the dashboard – *remember them?*

I drop ounces of cannabis in Urmston, Stockport and Salford.

Before I go, I give you the second bag of smack. 'Brown', you call it.

The plan is:

I score for you. You don't have to go out robbing while you cut down and stop.

*

I'm nearly asleep when you come into my room and get into my bed.

We haven't had sex for months but you seem to want me tonight.

I say, *You don't have to do that* – and you stop.

I tell you about a conversation I've had with a friend who says I'm not helping you, I'm killing you. 'Enabling' she calls it.

I say, *But if I don't help you, where will you go? And what about Jay-Jay?*

I realise you're asleep.

*

Your letter ends:

I know the screws are probably gonna read this, but here's what I'd do if you were here with me now…

I save that bit for later.

7.

This young guy on my wing sees the guitar I've borrowed from Education. Asks if I'll teach him some tunes.

He's kind of boyish, laughs a lot.

He says, *I'll pay you.*

I say, *You don't need to pay me!*

He points to a photo of you on my wall and says, *Your missus looks just like Nico.*

In his pad he's got material hanging on the walls and ceiling.

He says, *It's calico.*

When I play 'The Passenger' by Iggy Pop he goes nuts and dances about singing like Iggy.

DeNiro stops outside and gives me a glare that says, *Steer well clear of that guy!*

But Kenny's a good lad. I like him.

8.

My old mates from home write.

Yo dickhead! You were always a shit criminal!

Yo dickhead! I'm in a wheelchair. You went to university. Jus' sayin'.

Yo dickhead! What happened to your hero – Fidel What's-his-name? And that other guy you go on about.

He means Bobby Sands – the IRA hunger striker – who died in 1981 along with nine of his comrades. (*Realises.*) *I haven't even thought about poor Bobby for years!*

Yo dickhead! Three words. Bin. Liner. Skirt.

They mean well.

9.

Bron – short for Bronwyn – is coming out of the lift in Warrington, where he's come to get away from himself.

There's two guys shouting – which is just them laughing – and a *bang* – which is just a door closing – and there's a *flash* which only Bron sees – and he's back in the barracks near Belfast again – drinking with Billy and Tommy – when there's this – *snap!*

Like when you snap a ruler down on a desk.

Bron opens his eyes three weeks later and, *What's his mum doing there?*

She tells him the barracks was mortar bombed and Billy and Tommy are dead.

Bron's discharged from the army after that, but he can't work because of his drinking and fighting –

– And he's coming out of the lift – and two guys are shouting – and there's a *flash* – and one of the guys is dead.

Bron gets sixteen years for killing him.

He's got massive arms and uncool tattoos – and he's talking to a lad called Frankie who's got a typewriter in his pad – and he says,

Will you write a letter for me, Frankie? I'll pay you.

I say, *You don't need to pay me.*

DeNiro looks in and gestures, *Bron's sound.*

Bron's got a twinkle in his eye. *It's to the woman I'm shagging – Megan.*

And I know that name, do I...?

Miss Rosen.

My jaw drops.

Miss Rosen! The <u>screw</u>?

Bron's hopping up and down like a nine-year-old.

He's having sex with Miss Rosen?!

Whose bra strap – when you glimpse it under her clean, white shirt – when she's letting you into your pad – makes you sweat.

I put some paper in the typewriter. Vicariously.

What do you want to say to her, Bron?

You're the fucking writer, Frankie!

I ask him what he likes about her. Expecting body parts.

But he says, *It's the way she doesn't take shit off people. Especially not me. The way she makes me laugh without – whatsit? – deadpan, that's it. And sometimes when I talk to her on the landing she gives me this look and I swear she can see into me.*

I type it all in his voice and he loves it.

When he's gone I realise I've made another Big Mistake.

Miss Rosen's gonna know I know about them because of the typewriter!

Bron pokes his head back round.

By the way, DeNiro's giving me your book when he's read it. If it's as good as this, I can't wait!

Did I mention Bron's one of the jail's biggest enforcers?

10.

Dear Frankie...

(*Reliving his experience again...*)

St Anne's-on-Sea. South of Blackpool. Spooky as fuck.

Arms companies everywhere.

You look fantastic. Fresh out of rehab.

We go to the beach and Jay-Jay chases gulls on the mudflats in his undies.

You thank me for looking after Jay-Jay while you were in treatment.

This is me bringing him back to you. Four months later.

The evening sun catches your face and you say, *Where was Jay-Jay when customs raided?*

I tell you, by chance, he was on a sleepover and stayed till I got out on bail.

I <u>don't</u> tell you: some nights he was asleep on the back seat while I dropped ounces off in Urmston and Stockport and Salford.

You put your head on my shoulder and say, *You saved us.*

I feel like a fraud.

*

That night I make pasta and pesto while you put Jay-Jay to bed and read him a story.

His eyes shine as he listens to you.

As do yours.

Which makes me feel a bit better.

Later we talk about Jay-Jay and how mad it is being clean. Until it's dark and I can hardly see you against the street lights outside and you say,

Let's go to bed.

What happens next will always be there.

*

Afterwards, you tell me you love me and fall asleep in my arms.

I lie awake thinking about all the horrible stuff your stepdad did to you with his mates when you were a girl and I swear I'll never leave you.

*

(*Letter.*) *And I know the screws are going to read this but...*

Don't want to think about that now. (*Because of the stepdad stuff.*)

11.

Suddenly I'm ambushed by the past.

I'm playing Belfast Tony in the quarter-final of the chess competition.

Which is a big deal because the prize is two phone cards and a Mars bar.

He's massive. Twinkly eyes. But scary.

Do I say that about everyone?

The guy's slamming his pieces down like he's winning, but he's not.

I want to ask him where he's from. But that's awkward, too.

(*Because...*) The IRA are still going strong and where someone lives in Belfast can tell you which side they're on.

The plastic gangsters in here all side with the Loyalists of course.

For anyone who's too young to remember the Irish War – which is probably most of you because I'm such an old git:

The Loyalists – who the plastic gangsters love – are the Protestant fascist gangs.

Think: the EDL with machine guns and a hit list supplied by the police. Seriously.

The British press never call the Loyalists 'fascist', by the way – because that would make the IRA 'The Resistance'.

Instead they call the IRA 'terrorists'.

Which – to me – is like calling the French Resistance terrorists for fighting the Nazis. But: welcome to England.

Anyhow.

I finally pluck up the courage to ask – and Tony says, *I'm from West Belfast, just off the Falls. Do you know it?*

I say, *I was on an anti-internment march there.*

(*Explainer…*) Internment is when the British throw thousands of Catholics into a concentration camp and keep them there for years without trial.

I can tell Tony's impressed I know about internment.

But then he knocks his king over and stands up suddenly.

You sneaky wee bastard, you've beaten me! Typical English: Chat-chat-chat – stab you in the back. I should fucking kneecap you!

I'm about to say, *Okay you win* – when he laughs and says,

Your fucking face! Come for a walk round the wall.

12.

I'm embarrassed to admit I've always wanted to impress big men.

So now I'm trying to impress Belfast Tony with my knowledge of the Irish War.

I'm doing well so far. But when I name the ship carrying arms from Libya for the IRA – it was *The Eksund* – Tony says he's never met an English guy who knows so much.

Ha! All that time writing leaflets and articles no one ever read is paying off at last!

We talk for hours. Go out again after tea.

I realise I haven't talked about politics since I shut it all away, like a monster in a cave.

When I mention the miners' strike, Tony says,

The miners didn't lose their strike in the coal fields, Frankie. They lost it when the hunger strikers died four years before and the British workers didn't stop it.

I say, *First they came for the Irish...*

He says, *Dead on.*

Buzzing.

When I tell him it does my head in that most British socialists hate the IRA, he says,

The English wouldn't know a real revolution if it put them up against the wall and shot them.

I laugh. But realise he's serious and stop.

Then he says, *Only joking* and laughs.

I laugh again.

I'm a dickhead! (*For trying to impress him.*)

But I'm happy for once.

Probably because I don't know what's coming.

13.

Next day I see DeNiro coming out of Kenny's pad on the twos.

I thought he said to steer clear of Kenny?

He sees me looking. Pretends he doesn't. Saunters off.

Kenny comes out, waves *wait there*, grabs his guitar and belts out 'Venus in Furs' by The Velvets, writhing like Elvis.

Two Scousers on the ones stop and clap him, shaking their heads and laughing.

Kenny bows and shouts, *Elvis has left the building...!*

You've gotta love the guy.

14.

DeNiro appears in my doorway.

I read your book.

Oh shit.

He says, *It's good* – and stands there.

I say, *Thank you.*

He says, *Realistic.*

I say, *Do you think?*

He says, *The language is good.*

I say, *Thanks.*

He says, *It made me think.*

I wait.

He says, *The same thing happened to me, actually.*

I think I frown.

He nods. Kind of gently.

I say, *Did you pass it on to Bron?*

He says, *I don't think it's one for our Bronwyn. Do you?*

15.

I've been walking round the wall with Belfast Tony all week – loving it – when he asks me how an English dilettante gets interested in Ireland and the IRA.

I don't like the way he frames the question, obviously…

But I can tell him the exact moment.

*

(*Suddenly back there.*) The steps of the Student Union, Manchester.

The day before the end of the miners' strike.

Thatcher's Home Secretary – the twat in charge of policing the strike – is invited by the Conservative Student Society to give a talk.

Dickheads.

I'm still a student, but I'm hoping to get an article about the demo into *The Morning Star* because the editor said I 'write with the voice of the people'.

This is after I send him a story about my mate Jonno getting tasered in his wheelchair by cops who electrocute themselves because the bolt's touching the metal frame. Which Jonno says was well worth the fifty thousand volts.

Anyhow.

A few hundred of us are blocking the entrance to the union building – so Thatcher's big man has to go round the back like the beast he is.

The sun's shining.

There's socialists, anarchists, Jewish Students for Palestine.

The women's group are wearing tampon earrings to demand sanitary products on the NHS.

We're singing, shouting, laughing.

I'm puzzled by the Irish War at this point. I felt sorry for the hunger strikers, but I think:

If you attack the state, they're bound to come after you.

Then this.

Six riot vans pull up. The cops form a V – launch straight into us.

Kicking. Punching. Stamping.

I see my friend Mary grabbed by her hair. Lifted over a copper's head. Hurled to the ground. Kicked in the head.

Then. Out of a waiting car…

Home Secretary. Shoulders back. Marches up through the mayhem. In through the front door.

The cops arrest the kids they've beaten. Charge them with police assault. We form a committee to defend ourselves.

The chair of the committee – my mate – is followed by cops. Beaten by cops. They break into his house…

Then they take him to a local nick and rape him so violently he needs internal stitches.

But. Even as they launch into us. In that exact moment. I get it.

They attack you!

This is war!

Within a month I'm up to my neck in the worldwide revolution.

Chile, South Africa, Tamil Tigers, Palestine – it's all right there in Manchester.

16.

Next morning I go to the library to look up the word *dilettante*.

'A person who cultivates an area of interest, such as the arts, without real commitment'...?!

*

That night I imagine my old non-Western comrades reading my book.

All that stuff about drugs.

(*Cringe*.) *What have I become?*

17.

I sneak back to the wing from Education, to grab a snooze.

Miss Rosen's there. In her clean white shirt.

I pretend I haven't seen her, but she calls me over.

You'd better not be putting words in Bronwyn's mouth, Donnelly – or I'll maim you!

I say, *I just make it clear, miss. Honest. It's all him.*

She looks all soft, suddenly and says,

I couldn't make it out before. He can hardly write, the twat. Thank you.

Yess!

18.

Belfast Tony marches into my pad looking angry.

He says, *What are you in for, Frankie? And don't lie – the gym orderly can look you up on the computer.*

I tell him about the chocolate bars, trying to make myself sound clever. But he keeps going back over how it went wrong.

His tone is making me nervous.

I expain how the packages from Spain are sent to a place with multiple occupants, addressed to someone with a false name. We leave it for a week while someone who does lives there keeps an eye on it, so if it goes wrong they can say,

'Someone comes to pick up their post, officer. I don't know them, honest...'

Tony says, *But customs came to your house, Frankie. So the person at the other address must've told customs the package was meant for you?*

Oh shit. I suddenly know where this is going.

I tell him it was just this student lad I gave thirty quid to receive them.

Tony says, *So what happened to him, this grass? Is he in this nick?*

I deny it.

Why are you lying, Frankie? Why are you protecting a grass? I need a name. We can't have a grass on the loose.

He's in another nick, Tony.

No reason not to give me his name then.

I say, *I don't want anything to happen to him.* Which means he is in this nick – *Shit!*

Or was it you grassed him up, Frankie?

What? No! What is this, Tony?

He looks me dead-in-the-eye.

It's an interrogation, Frankie.

He lets that sink in.

I say, *Look, the guy is in this nick. We don't talk. And I'm the one who trusted him so, yes I'm protecting a grass. And I'm not giving you his name.*

Tony stands there staring at me.

For ages. Then he says,

Well done, Frankie. You can keep a secret. Now I know I can trust you. (*Laughing.*) *The face on you!*

I'm so relieved. But then I think, *Wait a minute!* And I say, *What are you in for, Tony?*

He looks angry again and says, *Nobody asks people that, Frankie.*

19.

I dodge into the gym to ask the orderly if he can look someone up on the computer for me.

The orderly's a con, by the way.

Rolo's so big he can hardly get his thighs under the desk.

He says, *Two cards.*

Meaning phone cards.

I snap two cards down.

Which kills me cos you're only allowed two cards a week from the canteen. The rest you have to hustle from drug dealers.

Rolo asks who I want to know about and when I tell him he frowns.

Two more cards.

Me and Josie already don't talk as much as we did. But I need to know!

Snap. Two more cards.

Rolo says, *No one asks about Belfast Tony. Now fuck off.*

Gutted!

I say, *Don't tell him I asked.*

He says, *Two cards.*

20.

I come out of my pad just in time to see Kenny smash his guitar over someone's head from behind.

Sounds like a Velvets riff.

The guy goes straight down. Kenny sees me.

(*Kenny – angry.*) *What?!*

I shrug. *Nowt.*

*

DeNiro calls me over.

I told you to steer clear of Kenny. The guy's a nonce.

I say, *He stabbed the guy who nonced him twenty-seven times!*

DeNiro says, *Do you want me to pass your book on to Bron?*

*

Ten minutes later Kenny comes into my pad saying he loved that guitar and can he have a hug.

I try to make it a quick one. But he won't let go and I realise he's crying.

I shut the door over with my foot.

After a bit he says, *You don't smell like my nana, but you do feel like her.*

I think that's a compliment.

I hold him tighter.

21.

Bron admits he's not actually shagging Miss Rosen.

The lads wouldn't understand what we <u>really</u> do, Frankie. Which is talk. About what happened to me in Ireland. And her family over there.

(Still Bron.) But then. This one night. After bang-up. She unlocks my door and just stands there on the landing. Staring at me. For ages.

(Still Bron.) I cried, Frankie. It was better than sex, I swear.

I'm typing it all in a letter to her when Belfast Tony looms in the doorway.

I've been feeling weird about having an ex-para in my pad since meeting Tony.

Tony says, *Is it you's the para?*

Bron says, *Aye. Till my mates were killed by a mortar bomb. Is it you, the Fenian fucker?*

Tony says, *Tell me this, para. If I was in the IRA and you were still in Belfast. Would you shoot me dead?*

Bron says, *Of course I fucking would!*

Tony steps forward smiling. *I like an honest man.*

They shake hands and I remember to breathe.

Tony says, *Is it loud in them troop carriers with a hundred kids hurling rocks at you?*

Bron says, *I pissed myself the first time. The lads called me Neptune after that, clever twats.*

Bron asks why Tony didn't join the IRA.

Tony says, *How do you know I didn't?*

Bron laughs and says Tony wouldn't be in a soft auld nick like this if he had. Which is true.

Bron tells Tony about Miss Rosen.

Tony says, *Risky for Megan! And for Frankie, with the typing an' all.*

Bron says, *I'm sorry, Frankie, I can be dangerous sometimes.*

Tony says, *So can I.*

*

When Bron goes Tony says, *Rolo tells me you were asking after me in the gym, Frankie.*

I say, *No?*

He says, *Don't lie. Ask me again if you like. Just be sure you wanna hear the answer.*

I don't ask.

He says, *Grow a pair, Frankie* – and goes.

22.

I'm chained on a long chain to Mr Scully in the hospital.

Real. Actual hospital. With nurses and human beings who walk around on their own.

Very <u>very</u> weird.

Especially chained to an old lech like Scully who's got bad breath and gives women marks out of ten as we pass.

As we come on to the ward I see you sitting there.

You nod, secretly.

Scully says, *Nine-and-a-half. Tattoo on her neck spoils it.*

This is a mad plan.

The jail doctor says if my housemaid's knee starts to hurt they can operate.

So – *Arrgh!*

Only question now is,

Will Scully sit there all night stinking and leching and ruin it?

He's talking to the nurse at the station. I'm chained to the bed. You're watching from the end of ward.

Next thing Scully unlocks me, says he's going home and if I'm not here in the morning I'll get two extra years – then goes.

Long live lazy bastard stinking horrible screws!

You're sitting next to me. We're holding hands and laughing.

Then the nurse comes over, draws the curtains round. Taps her watch and says,

You've got an hour.

And we're on the bed – and some of our clothes are off – and actually my knee does hurt a bit – so you go on top – which isn't my favourite – and we have to be quiet – and it's nice – obviously – but not how I imagined – and you really go for it – but you're not looking at me – so I touch your face – and I see it...

You don't want this.

You're not really here.

I try to stop you but you won't. And I realise...

You want this over with!

And it's tricky – but still a relief when it's done – and afterwards we talk – and you say it was lovely – but then you go and I'm devastated.

23.

Maybe it's because after you leave the hospital, I say yes to the pre-op and the post-op meds, when I should've phoned someone from NA…

Or maybe it's because when I get back to the wing I watch Levins get his ear ripped off for being a grass and nothing would make me look away…

Or maybe it's because I see Kenny run an errand for DeNiro that looks like a smack deal…

Which kills me!

Or maybe it's because I see Belfast Tony run an errand for DeNiro that's definitely a smack deal…

What the hell?!

Either way. Two minutes before bang-up. Two years since I last used. I score a wrap of heroin and shut myself in my pad…

Bang. (*Cell door.*)

*

I flatten the foil. Make a tooter.

I've seen you do it. I know how.

What am I doing?

On the bed. In the hospital.

Kill that feeling.

But wait.

Think!

In NA they say, *If you relapse, by the time you've actually scored it's too late.*

Great help. Thanks, guys.

I open the wrap. Put some on the foil. But,

How did I get <u>here</u>?

From <u>there</u>!

I see my old comrades. Back then. On marches. In meetings. How hard I try to be part of the fight against all this crap.

And then…

*

That fatal night.

Campaign Against the Poll Tax.

Big meeting. We're actually going to beat Thatcher on this one! Everyone knows it…

But afterwards. There's shouting in the car park. Excitement.

I go out. They've got a radio. Gathered round.

The Berlin Wall's coming down!

People are cheering and laughing.

I'm stunned. *Can't be!*

Am I the only person in the world who knows what that means?

I see one of my non-Western comrades.

He knows.

The Victory of Death.

Return of fascism.

Who'll stop it if the Soviets fall?

And they'll smash the welfare state now for sure!

The socialists go out to celebrate…

Along with Margaret Thatcher.

I crawl away like an exile.

I cave the monster. Take my place in the Great Silence.

Is that when I try crack for the first time?

It's everywhere by then.

I meet you for the first time the night the Soviets do fall.

Living in that truck. With your beautiful boy. Scoring off you.

(*Fade in mad/fantastic early-nineties rave music – getting louder – over…*)

I'm seeing us again now.

That place. The drive. The people. The nights.

Massive empty building.

You say 'take this' – (*A pill.*) and my belly thumps – there's so many of us – in this old factory – and the music! – coming up – all of us – I didn't know music could do this – and I remember…

Belonging again – being the same again – and the love – it feels so – like – love – and the drugs are – just – so – fucking good…!

(*For a moment we are lost in that mad, beautiful early-nineties house music – until it fades and* FRANKIE *is alone with the wrap of smack.*)

You were my drug then.

Best hit ever.

(*Realising more.*) But then – when you start on smack – the darkness.

*

(*Back to the here and now.*)

Fuck this! I screw up the stuff. (*Heroin and foil.*) Go over to the toilet…

But can't throw it in!

What's wrong with me?

My hand literally won't let go.

Perfect depiction of addiction.

Compromise.

I hide it in the cupboard. Go to the table. Write.

Dear Josie,

About the hospital.

(*Typing.*) *I know how you felt… I'm so sorry…*

But…

We have to fight for this!

24.

Next morning I'm on a mission.

No more Mr Soft Twat.

Kenny first.

I barge into his pad, *Are you working for DeNiro?*

Kenny says, *Chill out, what's it to you if I am?*

I say, *I'm worried about you.*

He says, *That's nice because people don't normally give a toss about me. Even my mum.*

I frown.

He says, *She stayed with him, you know.*

I say, *Who?*

He says, *The guy I stabbed.*

I say, *He's still alive?*

He says, *Only just. My mum said he had God on his side. The bastard.*

I say, *Are you having sex with DeNiro?*

He nods.

I say, *Do you like it?*

He says, *No, and he makes me look after his stuff. I've got all the heroin in the nick in my pad!*

I say, *What's in it for you, Kenny?*

He says, *People think I'm a nonce. DeNiro protects me.*

I say, *DeNiro <u>tells</u> people you're a nonce. You need to stand up for yourself!*

Kenny laughs and says, *We should start the revolution, man –* and his eyes shine with the thought of it.

*

Next up. Belfast Tony.

I knock on and say, *What are you in for, Tony?*

He says, *At last, cojones!*

He comes to the door, checks about. Says,

Sit down.

25.

Thirty miles away.

A young woman with a tattoo on her neck settles down to write a letter she's been meaning to write for too long.

Dear Frankie...

*

Tony says, *I'm coming through customs in Hull when they lift me and I think, 'I'm done for'...*

I've got thirty years hanging over me, Frankie. Thirty years for something that was a big deal in England. Military target. That you definitely know about.

(*Frankie, out.*) ...Which, even if he told me what it was, I wouldn't tell you lot because I'm not a grass, yeah?

*

Dear Frankie,

Josie writes a few lines. Screws it up. Starts again.

*

(*Tony.*) *I'm travelling on my brother's passport. I look just like him...*

He's never been 'involved', my brother. But he has a fight with a peeler when he's drunk in Manchester...

And now this cop's in Hull and he thinks I'm my brother...!

*

Dear Frankie,

I meant to tell you in the hospital but...

No. (*Screws it up again.*)

*

(*Tony.*) *...So I have to plead guilty to something stupid my brother did, because it's better to do six as an 'Ordinary Decent Criminal' – than thirty for what I <u>really</u> did...*

...So that's what I'm in for.

I say, *Thanks for telling me.*

But he's not done.

*

Dear Frankie,

Please don't hate me...

*

(Tony.) If we lose this war now, Frankie, it'll be another hundred years of the Irish leaving Ireland – and even the protestants'll get it in the end...

I mean, where are the shipyards now? And the factories they kill us to get the best jobs in...?

*

Dear Frankie,

You're a lovely guy and I really love you...

*

(Tony.) We're still standing, Frankie – we're still a force...

...But there's bad stuff going on with this 'peace process' shite.

I mean what does 'peace' even mean to the people at the bottom? Is <u>this</u> peace, Frankie? In here? All this thieving and fighting over scraps...?

*

Dear Frankie,

You saved us. But...

*

(Tony.) I need to get back to Belfast to have my say, Frankie. If ya know what I mean...?

I say, *You want me to help you escape?*

He goes, *Shh* – and nods.

I say, *But I thought you worked for DeNiro now?*

He says, *Of course not! The guy's a drug dealer!*

I know he's lying now.

So I get up and say, *I can keep a secret, don't worry. But no.*

26.

When the mail trolley comes there's a letter from you.

Dear Frankie... I've met someone.

I stay in my pad for three weeks and don't come out.

Dear Frankie...

You say the guy's nice and he loves Jay-Jay, but I still want to kill him.

Dear Frankie...

And over and over in my head there's this thought...

(*The thought:*) *...There's a way out in my cupboard.* (*The heroin.*)

27.

Bron comes in and says, *Take down the photos.*

I take down the photos.

*

Kenny comes in with a guitar and asks me to teach him something new.

I say no.

*

DeNiro pokes his head round and says, *Are you okay for sugar?*

I nod.

*

Footsteps.

My door opens.

Miss Rosen.

She says, *Write yourself a letter, Frankie.*

*

Three whole weeks.

Then Kenny comes back and says he finished my book – and he got a hard-on in the sex scene.

I laugh for the first time.

He says, *I've written my own story, can I show it ya?*

I shrug.

He goes to the door – closes it – undoes his trousers.

What the fuck are you doing, Kenny?!

I'm showing you my story. Look.

Suddenly I'm looking at his thigh.

Which has no hair on it at all.

Just this line of thin white scars running up the inside – which he runs his finger over.

Some of them are new.

I stare at the scars, feeling weird because they look exactly like Josie's.

He says, *You won't find this one in the library, will you.*

Then he asks if I'll teach him something new now.

I say, *Okay, but there's something I need you to throw down the toilet for me.*

When he sees what it is, he says, *Where did you get heroin from?*

I say, *Where do you think?*

He says, *DeNiro's a bastard!*

28.

The next day there's this scream on the twos – and a sound like a knife being scraped along a wall.

Kenny's slashed DeNiro's cheek from his mouth to his ear.

We see it flopping about as DeNiro bolts down the stairs bleeding everywhere.

Next thing, there's like this – *Puffff…*

A cloud of brown dust explodes over the balcony and Kenny's there like Christ the Redeemer – empty plastic bag in hand – singing 'I'm So Free' by Lou Reed!

As if by ancient force, junkies appear and stare in wonder as the cloud of magic dust settles at their feet.

Then they get down on their knees and sniff and snort and feel the love of Jesus coursing through them.

One of the junkies salutes Kenny. (*Fist salute.*)

Kenny shouts, *This is the revolution, man!*

I look over and see Belfast Tony staring at me.

*

By the time I get up there, Kenny's rocking on his bed.

I'm careful not to step in the blood.

I say, *You've got to go on the numbers, Kenny!*

Meaning: 'Rule forty-three. Prisoners isolated for their own protection.'

...Like, right now!

He says, *No way, man* – and points at the calico.

Red stars everywhere. *Jesus!*

I sit down next to him.

He says, *Do you really like me, Frankie? Or do you just want sex?*

I say, *I don't want sex!* Even though it did cross my mind one night.

He says, *After my nana, I like you the best out of anyone.*

I say, *You're a good lad.*

He says, *I'm definitely not that.*

I say, *It depends on your definition of good* – and he laughs.

He says, *Promise you'll write about me one day?*

I say, *I will if you promise to go on the numbers.*

He says, *I thought you understood. I'm a motherfucking free man!*

29.

I knock on Belfast Tony's door.

I say, *I know you work for DeNiro. I know you lied about it. But if you stop him taking revenge on Kenny, I'll help you escape.*

He looks very dark and says, *Do you know who I fucking am? You don't talk to me like that.*

I say, *For all I know, you're a lying fucking gangster like the rest of them.*

I see it land. But I don't care any more.

He's staring at me.

I brace myself.

He stands up. Looking like a soldier.

He says, *I'll have a word with DeNiro.*

I walk away – and realise I've done a little wee in my pants.

30.

The next day they don't let us out after lunchtime bang-up and I get a bad feeling.

There's screws on Kenny's landing.

I'm peering through the door crack.

I see them go past.

Kenny's been found hanging in his pad.

*

It goes down as suicide.

31.

A week later. I haven't moved from my bed. Belfast Tony appears.

He says, *It wasn't DeNiro did that to your wee friend.*

I shrug.

He says, *Sit the fuck up when I'm talking to you!*

I sit up.

He says, *The man's heartbroken. He lost his looks and his boyfriend all in one go.*

I don't laugh.

He says, *There's people in here want to impress the guy. Your wee friend had no chance against all this.*

I sit there while he shuts the door over.

He says, *I tried, Frankie. Now what about ye?*

I say, *All the years I've supported the struggle in Ireland all anyone says is, 'The IRA are gangsters', 'The IRA are drug dealers'. I see you working for DeNiro and I'd rather you were lying about your brother and Hull and you were an Ordinary Decent Criminal like the rest of us.*

He says, *I can't believe I'm taking this off a fucking dilettante. I've taken a massive risk on you!*

I say, *Are they right, though?*

He says, *There's no heroin in our areas in the north of Ireland, thanks to us. Even the Brits accept that. You know what we do to the dealers. Everyone does – (Kneecap gesture.) We're a guerrilla army, Frankie, you know we are.*

I say, *I don't know what to believe any more.*

He says, *You're brave to challenge me on it. We're supposed to set an example in British jails. I let myself down. But no one knows who I am here – except you. And this is England. It's everyone against everyone here. It eats your soul...*

(Still Tony.) And to be honest, Frankie, I need ketchup and phone cards like the rest of yous.

Still not laughing.

He says, *You're a communist. How did you end up dealing?*

I say, *I keep trying to work it out. But. I think. Honestly. When the Soviet Union collapsed, I lost hope.*

He laughs. *Oh, so you say, 'Communism's dead, pass the fucking crack pipe?'*

I can't help myself. I say, *It means you're going to lose, Tony. In Ireland.*

He says, *Stand up and say that to me again!*

I stand up and say, *Even if you win a military victory – where will you turn to for help? They'll crush you.*

Jesus Christ, did you work that out with a pencil, Frankie! In Ireland we marched for jobs and votes and they bombed us and shot us and burned us out – and then the Brits came to help them. We're fighting for our lives. Not for some – psychological – fucking – fix! Is that what you want, Frankie? You want me to help you with your brain? Is that what revolution is to you?

I say, *No, that's exactly why I walked away!*

He says, *Rise above yourself, Frankie! Like your wee mate did in his own mad way. Like everyone who takes a stand. It's your choice. Just be glad you've got one.*

32.

Typewriter.

(*Typing a letter to himself.*)

Dear Frankie,

Did Kenny do that because of your words?

Dear Frankie,

You told him to stand up for himself. And he did.

Dear Frankie,

Are you going to put your money where your mouth is?

Dear Frankie,

When are you going to stand the fuck up again?

For real this time.

Not just for the fix.

I rip the letter up. Flush it. March down the landing to Belfast Tony's pad.

I say, *Looks like you're going to have to rely on a dilettante to help you.*

But also point out my lack of a right hook.

He says. *It's not that. You're English. You don't take drugs. When was the last time you had a pad spin?*

I say, *They never search my pad.*

He says, *They spin mine all the time.*

And I get it.

I say, *Okay then.*

He says, *Someone'll bring you something. Put it in your cupboard. Don't touch it.*

33.

Two nights later. Two hours after bang-up. Footsteps.

My door opens.

Miss Rosen again.

I've been thinking about her a lot lately.

In my loneliness.

She steps inside. Comes right in…!?

She undoes her jacket. Pulls out a cloth bag.

Something heavy. Puts it in my cupboard.

A gun?

What the hell?!

She looks at me and says, *Don't touch it.*

I feel like I'm dreaming.

I say, *Is he blackmailing you? Belfast Tony? It was Bron told him about the the letters, not me.*

She shakes her head. *Is that what you think of me? I'd only do this if I was being blackmailed?*

She says, *My family's Irish. I've got cousins involved. We're everywhere, Frankie. It's why we're still standing after twenty years.*

Then she winks and goes.

And it hits me.

Terror.

34.

Next morning in the queue for breakfast I see Tony looking at me and nod.

He looks away.

*

I shit myself all day and the next night – but nothing happens!

*

The next night's worse.

I could get ten years for this!

No, wait…!

If he shoots a screw and they trace it to me...? That's life, isn't it...?

I could say I was forced into it.

What the hell!?– No!

Don't even think it!

Say nothing.

Know nothing.

Hold your nerve.

I don't hold my nerve.

But I don't do anything stupid.

For once.

And I realise,

This is what it feels like to have something to lose.

This is why people only fight when they've got nothing to lose.

I knew it. But now I <u>know</u> it.

I embrace the pain.

Take it to heart.

And I promise. If I get out of this...

I will remember.

35.

Twenty minutes before bang-up next night, Tony appears. Checks about. Steps in.

He says, *There was a hitch. And they gave my pad a spin, so you saved me.*

He opens the cupboard and says. *Did you touch it?*

I say, *Of course I fucking did!*

He says, *I'll give it a wipe.*

Then he stands up and says, *Why did you do it, Frankie? Was it something I said?*

I want to say, *Because I didn't know it was going to be a gun!*

But actually…?

I say, *Because this isn't peace. And it never will be.*

Tony says, *Good work, comrade,* and goes.

36.

Two a.m. As pre-arranged. Miss Rosen answers Tony's emergency bell with Mr Scully. The dirty stinking lech.

Tony takes them to reception at gunpoint where he announces he's a member of the Provisional IRA and if everyone does exactly as they're told they won't be harmed and neither will their families.

They take the hint.

Tony walks out the gate. Gets in a waiting car. Vanishes.

The CCTV goes missing.

The screws get thirteen weeks' paid leave to recover.

Miss Rosen spends three, very sunny, months in Thailand.

So Bron tells me.

*

I go back to Education and write every day for the rest of my sentence.

I also get my head kicked in trying to stop a grass get a beating. Plus a crack on the head and week on the block for standing up to a screw – and I get a black eye breaking up a fight.

I can't keep my mouth shut any more. The monster's woken up again.

Oh. And – (*By the way.*) I'm writing about Kenny.

37.

Epilogue.

Kenny's nana scatters Kenny's ashes on the beach at Formby on a day when the sun glints off the water.

Then she walks in the woods nearby where the red squirrels are and cries her eyes out.

*

When I get out I *do* remember.

I stand on the corner of a Saturday selling a communist newspaper with my non-Western comrades, telling people, *If you can't fight yourself, stand by the people who have to.*

*

Flash forward.

Bron gets out. Kills a man. Goes back to jail.

*

Flash forward.

Josie's here with her wife, dropping Jay-Jay off for the weekend.

He's fourteen now and has to put up with my two young daughters doting on him.

But my oldest also lectures him on the importance of recycling when he puts his pizza box in the wrong bin.

*

Flash forward.

I'm fifty-eight years old.

It's the end of the era that started with the fall of the Berlin Wall.

I write a short story for an anthology, but I'm advised to delete some lines or risk jail under the new terrorism laws.

*

Flash forward.

I'm on an anti-fascist demo with my daughters.

My oldest spends six months in Palestine fighting illegal house demolitions by Israeli settlers – and when she leads the chanting sometimes I burst into tears.

Today she's pushing Jonno up the High Road in his wheelchair and they're making a right noise.

The march is massive and my youngest is holding a banner ten times bigger than herself, standing on a bridge – smiling and shouting to us below – looking like Christ the Redeemer.

And there's flags and drums and laughing and raised fists – and people are screaming suddenly – and there's a roar – and people are flying – and – I'm hit by a van a racist's driven at us – and I die at the side of the road.

SANCTUARY

Ed Edwards

A short play, commissioned by HOME MCR for the thirty-fifth anniversary of the deportation of Viraj Mendis.

Viraj died on 16 August 2024.

This version of the piece was performed on 1 March 2025, by Eve Steele at the memorial service for Viraj in the Church of the Ascension, Hulme, Manchester – where Viraj took sanctuary all those years ago.

Special thanks to Father Azariah France-Williams, Rector of Ascension Church, Hulme and Kerry Pimblott of the Race, Roots and Resistance Collective and Lisa Allen, now at Shakespeare North, for their hard work and loving commitment in bringing Viraj and his sanctuary back to public consciousness.

Notes on the Text

One actor.

Bare stage.

Direct address in plain text.

Dialogue or thoughts in italics.

The freedom song was sung by a choir recruited from the audience and participants and taught before the performance.

The song itself is 'Umkhonto we Sizwe'.

Original lyrics in Zulu: Hamba kahle Umkhonto weSizwe / Thina bant' abamnyama siz' misele ukuwabulala wona lama bhulu.

A performance of the song can be heard here: youtu.be/br_i1UsNJx0

1.

Warnings.

One. The following piece is based on the writer's experiences as a young man in his twenties. I'm not a young man in my twenties. Sorry about that!

Two. This is a drama. Or is it a poem? A lament maybe.

The point is, it's not a documentary…

So we've changed some characters and made some characters up from a mix of others. Because there were so many people involved and this has to be short.

We haven't changed Viraj and his partner Karen, obviously.

So don't sue the writer, yeah?

Anyway they've cut legal aid for the likes of you, so he's not worried.

Basically this is an attempt to capture something of the impossible task we set ourselves that came to an end thirty-six years ago.

The task that Viraj Mendis set us.

It's the truth according to Ed and no one else.

Three. There are three swear words which Father Azariah has okayed.

We dropped one because as Father Azariah pointed out, it was well-gratuitous!

Let's begin.

2.

1985. Manchester.

There's a woman speaking. Brenda Downes. From Belfast.

Brenda's angry and no one in this echoey old hall is surprised.

Her husband is dead. He was twenty-four years old.

Do you know what a plastic bullet is? Brenda says. *Sounds harmless, doesn't it!*

She pulls something white out of her handbag and hurls it across the hall we're in.

The sound is unforgettable.

I can still hear it all these years later as it crashes like a rock along the wooden floor.

We've heard of plastic bullets. Now we know what they are.

Brenda's husband is shot at point-blank range. The cop gets off scot-free.

People cheer Brenda and shout, *Get out of Ireland!* and, *Shame!*

Brenda raises her fist in that salute we used to see everywhere, but see less now.

When she's done, a shy man shuffles to the front to talk about his anti-deportation campaign.

His stutter is profound – but he pledges solidarity to Brenda and people take the time to listen to him.

I buy the newspaper he's selling.

This is the first time I meet Viraj Mendis.

I've heard of Viraj. And his paper. Someone with no axe to grind says it's the best paper on the left.

I take it home and read an article that says,

Fidel Castro calls Ronald Reagan a madman and a bum.

And I'm all in.

3.

Time passes.

I'm outside a church in Hulme.

There's banners and a crowd of people and I'm told something special is gonna happen.

But not what.

There's Anwar Dita – who Bobby Sands wrote a poem for – and someone from the Tamil Tigers and Anti-Fascist Action.

I don't remember how I even know Chairman Martin who sells the same paper as Viraj. But when he asks me to be there that day I know I have to come.

There's shouting and a megaphone and cheers and the anger is kind of happy.

Chairman Martin is talking and there's a priest and Martin says,

(*Megaphone.*) *Viraj Mendis is taking sanctuary in this church today and won't come out until he's won the right to stay in this country no matter how long that takes!*

Everyone cheers and what a sight they all are in the cold with their banners and the drums and the singing – because they're all singing now.

It's a South African freedom song that sounds amazing because Andrea's leading it like she does, even though I don't know who Andrea is yet.

And they all march into the church to plan what to do to keep Viraj safe from fascists and fight the Home Office…

And I am all in.

4.

Two years pass.

The phone goes. No mobiles back then.

A voice says, *The church! They're raiding the church!*

The phone tree has been activated.

There's a system. It's always been there. Since that first day.

If they come – the fascists or the cops – one call from the church sets it off.

I phone you and two other people and set off down there.

You phone three other people and set off down there.

The branches spread out from the trunk.

We are a forest!

Friday night, six p.m.

Twelve riot vans pull up outside the church.

Well, not <u>outside</u>. They can't pull up outside. It's pedestrianised back then.

That's their problem.

They have to get from the end of the street to the church.

And back.

Two hundred yards.

Imagine the Home Office if they fumble this!

The eyes of the whole country are on this now.

Viraj and his soldiers have made sure of that.

Within twenty minutes we are three-hundred strong and there's shouting and singing and the anger is no kind of happy.

Twelve giant blue cockroaches parked at the top versus us, the people.

And we're all in now.

*

But this is <u>not</u> the end.

The cockroaches drive away and we cheer!

False alarm? Have we won?

Is this it?

We don't know it yet, but we haven't won. This is the beginning of the end.

I know it now, so I go back.

In time.

To find the good things – or something funny to remember all of this by.

Good first.

5.

Cathy finds us.

When you see her on the desk by the main entrance to the church – where she's always on the rota now – she seems older than her years.

One day she's just there.

She's sixteen years old and she's all in right away.

She makes milky tea for the old women who come in to pray and do the flowers in the church and they smile at Cathy and tell her she's a lovely girl.

Cathy says, *Hello, Mrs Lewis, how's your old mum?*

And, *Do you want anything from the shops later?*

Andrea tells me Cathy's in care. Or was. But now she's just always here on the rota.

All I ever wanted was a family, Cathy says, meaning us. The campaign.

There always has to be two people on the rota to start the phone tree if anything happens – day and night – but Cathy's doing too much.

Like everyone does when they first come along.

But Cathy doesn't burn out. She's there most days for a whole year.

And then there's Cillian with his flashing eyes and his wicked grin.

Cillian who makes Cathy laugh with his stories about Ireland and robbing and his battered-looking van that he parks on the front instead of at the back.

Cillian's only eighteen but looks thirty. In a good way. (*Wink*.)

And now Cathy's pregnant, and flashing eyes and good stories don't mean you'll make a good dad. So everyone thinks this is a disaster.

Except Cathy.

And Cillian.

And Mrs Lewis actually who says, *You'll make a lovely mum, dear.*

Cathy smiles and pats her belly. *All I ever wanted was a family.*

But then Cillian disappears – but Cathy's friend Blond Jonny, who's seventeen and as punky as Sid Vicious, steps in.

Punky Jonny's quiet and thinks about things and suddenly he's the one with Cathy, even though Cathy's about as punky as your aunty Irene from Wigan.

So it's always Cathy and Jonny on the rota now – and Cathy's getting bigger and everyone thinks this'll end badly. Even Mrs Lewis.

But they're wrong.

Cathy has three children to Punky Jonny before she's twenty-two, plus Cillian's one. And Jonny's a full-time dad to them all and Cathy gets a job in the council and they're still together now to this day.

So that's the first four of the eleven campaign babies that are born because Viraj Mendis goes into sanctuary.

They're all grown up now.

Even Cillian.

*

That's one of the good things.

That's beautiful.

6.

We're on Market Street petitioning for Viraj.

Some of us are selling papers too.

Sign a petition for Viraj Mendis...?

You sign... there...

And then there's a box that says, *Contribution.*

Some people tut at the box. But most give you a quid and the campaign needs the money for the coach to London for the Judicial Review.

It's Viraj's last legal option.

Where we'll make a right noise.

Sign a petition for Viraj Mendis please...

Uh-oh! Inspector Mallard at two o'clock – (*Direction of approach.*) With two of his uniformed cronies...

In my mind it's always Inspector Mallard.

Squat little cop with a red face and a cliché tache.

He can't believe his luck today because there's only six of us.

You can't sell papers on this street, he says.

Anticipatory pleasure scrunched on his blotchy face.

Normally the poor guy has to contend with our marches and public events when we're an army and he gets flustered when we don't obey his orders, or invent cheeky workarounds.

He can't help himself.

We are Chaos. He is Order.

Once, when we're arguing with his superior officer in Bootle Street Police Station over our plans to march two thousand people down Deansgate on a busy Saturday afternoon with an Irish Republican drum and pipe band, Mallard grumpily interjects – but his superior officer shouts,

Be quiet, Mallard, I'll deal with this! (*To us.*) *It's fine. It's a free country. Do what you like.*

We laugh for a week about Mallard's face that day.

(*The face.*)

But now it's his turn.

I say, *What law says we can't petition here?*

Mallard says, *I didn't say you can't <u>petition</u> here. It's selling those.* Meaning the papers.

He quotes the local licencing law verbatim and I'm impressed.

He says, *You can sell them on Tib Street if you like.*

I say, *There's no one on Tib Street!*

He says, *That's as maybe.*

And it's his day today. We both know it.

<u>Except</u>…

Except for beautiful. Handsome. Older. Communist…

Alexander.

Who's come up from London to be with the campaign as it nears its climax. From the communist group Viraj is a member of. Who plans everything with Viraj in minute detail…

… And whose beautiful, handsome, Armenian voice booms out suddenly behind Mallard. Like Lenin on Market Street.

Comrades and friends – people of Manchester – please witness this officer obstructing our freedom of speech! Is this not a free country? Are we not allowed to debate politics on the streets of this country any more? People of Manchester! Witness this act of political repression...

Alexander is a volcano, but somehow polite and old-fashioned too.

Mallard is stunned. His mouth's moving but – (*Not saying anything.*)

I feel sorry for him. Almost.

Do we live in a police state now…? Alexander is asking the slightly bewildered-but-definitely-growing crowd.

I say to Mallard, *We'll just petition for now, yeah?* To give him an out.

Which we both know is nonsense. But he takes anyway.

We watch him strut away, muttering into his moustache, Alexander's gorgeous voice still ringing in his ears.

You can almost hear an, *I'll be back.* (*Schwarzenegger.*)

We already loved Armenian Alexander. He's our dad now.

And Viraj is our leader.

7.

It's hard to get politics into drama.

Believe me I've tried. You can get one or two facts into a play, three max.

Because drama has to be about character and feeling.

Except with Viraj, his character is the politics.

I spend two years of my life fighting for Viraj who never leaves the church.

I see him giggle like a seven-year-old at daft jokes. And good ones. Shoulders going, the lot.

I see him gloomy and down, staring at the ground, tapping his foot, blinking furiously while we, the campaign committee, argue over his fate.

I see him silent as night while his partner rages and shouts at the world and at us, the committee.

Viraj can hardly speak for his shy stammer but I see his bearded face appear over the wall at the back of the church to address a crowd of three thousand people gathered in the car park after a march.

I see his clever eyes follow every nuance and twist of every meeting. Like his life depends on it.

I see him accept a vote over a campaign plan he disagrees with, even though his life depends on it.

I see how much everyone loves him.

I see how much his partner loves him.

I see Viraj live for two years with zero privacy.

We, his comrades, see it all.

But in two years of fighting I never once sit down and have a private conversation with him.

I don't need to.

He's all in and so are we.

8.

So here's your three facts.

It should take about forty seconds.

i The Tamil people are a desperately oppressed minority in the north and east of Sri Lanka which used to be called Ceylon.

ii Sri Lanka is an ex-British colony off the coast of India whose government and army are still totally dependent on the British. You know the score.

iii Led by their revolutionary army – the Tamil Tigers – the Tamil people have risen up to create a safe homeland for themselves in the north and east, but they're being slaughtered, in their tens of thousands, by a ruthless and bloodthirsty Sri Lankan army determined to stop the Tamils at any cost.

Got it?

Viraj is a known supporter of the Tamil Tigers.

If he's deported back to Sri Lanka he could be killed like the tens of thousands already dead.

But the British Home Office don't care about that.

They say, *'Mendis has nothing to fear in Sri Lanka'. 'Sri Lanka is a democracy.'*

They say Viraj is making it up because he wants to stay in Britain.

They also deny their links to the murderous regime in Sri Lanka.

But the irony is, it's not even about Sri Lanka for the Home Office.

Not really.

It's about the immigration laws.

At this moment they're locking down Europe against migrants for the beginning of the future we're now in.

It's due to start in 1992. It's called *Fortress Europe*. And Viraj is in the way of the juggernaut.

<u>We're</u> in the way of the juggernaut.

If they let him stay it messes with their plans for the fortress wall.

Some people support Viraj because he could be killed in Sri Lanka.

It's why the church say yes to sanctuary.

The hard core support him because we're against the immigration laws.

I feel guilty sometimes because I care more about that side of it.

But the immigration laws are essential to the exploitation of the poor countries by the rich.

Because, when we steal the wealth of the poor nations, we have to make sure the poor don't follow their own money here.

Our fat Western life depends on their exclusion.

As a communist and anti-imperialist Viraj is against the immigration laws too.

Of course he is.

But like most asylum seekers , Viraj is also against the immigration laws because his life depends on it.

Like I say, his character and his politics are the same.

So, *Fuck the immigration laws!*

And fuck the Home Office!

A victory for Viraj is a victory for the world!

Viraj knows it.

We know it.

They know it.

*

How many people can a juggernaut crush before it grinds to a halt?

We'll see.

9.

Andrea is teaching us a South African freedom song…

It's the one they sing at funerals for fallen comrades fighting apartheid.

(*SING a couple of rounds of the call and response.*)

The first time we're arrested together we sing this song in the van on the way to Bootle Street police station.

There's four of us in the back, stamping our feet, rocking the van. Literally.

(*SING the same song much faster and harder – clapping the beat defiantly now for a couple of rounds.*)

Imagine the van stopped at traffic lights rocking like a shipwreck.

Cops looking embarrassed.

Another one of the good things.

We're arrested a few times during the two years it takes Viraj to exhaust all his legal options.

'Disturbing the peace.' 'Obstructing the highway.' That sort of stuff.

Every time we fight them in court.

Every time we win.

And everyone learns you can win.

Except…

Except for this one time.

Six of us have been arrested.

Six of us are found guilty.

Six of us appeal, but only five of us get off.

And the only person to lose…?

Even though we're all up on exactly the same charge…?

Andrea. The only one on this arrest who's black.

Andrea gets a month in Styal women's nick. Everyone else walks.

(*Two last angry rounds of our song. The second one quiet for next line…*)

Viva Andrea! Who taught this very shy person to sing their flipping heart out!

10.

By the time the end comes there's a huge mix of people gathered around Viraj.

You could call us diverse.

You could call us a rabble.

A Rabble Army who can perform impossible tasks.

You see, what Viraj is doing here really…

What Viraj and his communist comrades really want…

Is to create warriors.

Viraj sets the challenge…

Goes into sanctuary…

Which means two people on the rota every day and a minimum of four people <u>every night</u> for <u>two years</u> from a handful of volunteers…

It's impossible. But we do it anyway.

We respond and grow our capabilities.

And then, halfway through <u>this</u> impossible task…

We vote to march every Friday night from the city centre to the church till Viraj has won.

And probably to show I'm a fully-fledged warrior myself now, I volunteer to organise this impossible task.

Which is how I get to be such good mates with Inspector Mallard. (*Wink*.)

But sometimes…

On the Friday night march, or at a rally, or in a meeting – how to describe it…?

I'm just not this individual me any more…

*

We're an army…

Of the Clever and the Daft.

Of the Beautiful and the Troubled.

The Lost and the Lonely.

The Holy and the Sinners…

We're more than ourselves.

In this church where,

Cathy meets Cillian.

And Jonny.

And I smoke less weed, often almost none.

We are council workers.

Students.

Teachers.

Unemployed.

We're homeless.

Old.

We're ex-cons who've spent over half our life in jail.

Probation officers.

Christians.

We're secretly drinking.

We work as a receptionist in a gay brothel where someone you wouldn't expect comes in for a punt.

…Someone who's a bit nicer to us now.

In a few years' time we'll be found dead in a flat that was just over there. Strung out on heroin.

We're a respectable church-going man who is not young any more who falls in love with a Scottish lad with sad eyes and a cute smile and we go on our first ever demo with him.

We join the campaign for all the wrong reasons.

Sometimes even just to keep warm in winter.

We're inspired by communists like Viraj and Armenian Alexander.

We're frustrated by the ones who just try to recruit us.

We – okay so this one's an 'I' – I don't feel good enough to be a proper communist.

(*Moving on…*) We talk too much in meetings.

We get angry when Chairman Martin shuts us up. But later in the pub we're fine.

We resent Viraj for taking over our church, but after a talk with Father John we pray for him sincerely.

We fall out bitterly when some of the women want to break away and form their own section. But later in the pub we're fine.

We say we'll do something for the campaign but don't and stay away for ages out of shame.

We come back and people are thrilled to see us again.

We don't cut our hair for ten years after Bobby Sands dies on hunger strike in an Irish jail and swear that if anyone comes for Viraj we'll kill them and mean it literally.

We're a lovely, devout woman who is heartbroken for Viraj and struggles to believe this can happen in a Christian country.

We're a local youth who fires off a machine gun in the car park behind the pub down the road.

We move to Manchester to be part of this and stay for the rest of our lives.

We will remember for the rest of our lives the moment we stand up to a cop and they don't know what to do because we have our comrades with us.

We have eleven flipping babies!

An – 'I' again –

I find out later it's different to be arrested for a real crime. No one outside singing your name now.

But no matter who we are before – or later – we'll go on a demo in London or Manchester – or even Clitheroe where the Minister for Immigration lives – and we'll feel the drums and see the banners and raise our fist and shout like we've never shouted,

Viraj Mendis Will Stay!

And we'll know what it is to have comrades.

*

And then the catastrophe.

11.

The first sign of it is a secret message from the Home Office.

They're clever bastards at the Home Office.

Thatcher and her cronies have been fighting tougher nuts than us for a decade now.

We have study groups to analyse it all.

In their first attack they kill ten hunger strikers in Ireland.

They fight against revolutions in South Africa, Tamil Eelam, Chile, El Salvador, Afghanistan, Nicaragua, everywhere there *is* one.

They've backed murderous gangs in Africa who've killed and raped their way around Namibia, Angola and Mozambique, burning schools and health centres. Any symbol of progress for new-born revolutions – *bang.*

They've crushed the strongest union in Britain.

And now it's our turn.

This tiny immigration campaign in a church in Hulme.

Chairman Martin says, *We had a visit from the Bishop of Manchester today with a message from the Home Office.*

This is a closed meeting of the campaign committee, upstairs. Near the room where Viraj has spent the last two years.

Where Tony Benn and Jeremy Corbyn come to speak privately to Viraj and the committee.

Where one night we find Viraj's partner, Karen, alone, crying that Viraj is going to die and she can't live without him.

Where we sleep on the overnight rota.

Where Cillian and Cathy first kiss.

Where I won't set foot for thirty-five years and when I do I burst into tears.

Where someone from the church tells me recently that all the church's papers about Viraj and sanctuary were destroyed.

Where today downstairs there is a thriving foodbank.

It's the beginning of the end.

Viraj looks tense.

Karen looks like she's wants to scream.

The House of Lords have rejected the final appeal from the Judicial Review.

The only option for the Home Office now is to raid the church, or grant Viraj special leave to remain which will mess up Fortress Europe and which they will never in a hundred years do.

Or…

Martin says, *The Home Office say Viraj can go to any third country that will take him.*

It's a compromise which keeps Fortress Europe safe because it doesn't establish a precedent.

And of course Viraj has to take it.

It's a victory – of sorts – isn't it?

Did we tame the beast?

Or is it a trap?

If we say yes, will they take it as a sign of weakness and raid the church?

We can work that out as we go.

First let's keep Viraj safe.

*

But Friday…

Twelve giant cockroaches up the street, full of cops.

Phone tree activated.

We're three-hundred strong.

The singing is no kind of happy…

They drive off…?

*

Two days later it comes.

12.

Crash – police!

Footsteps – banging – shouting.

Dawn raid.

Still dark.

Uniformed men know exactly where to go.

Boots thunder up stone stairs.

A sledge hammer crashes on the door of the sacristy.

Viraj inside.

Empty church hall echoes to the sound of desecration.

The door's in.

Viraj is shouting. He's chained himself to the radiator.

Karen is screaming, shaking, watching.

Viraj is roughly cut free and bundled down the stairs. His arm is nearly broken.

Karen stares in terror. Powerless.

Viraj is marched down the street.

Shoved in a police car.

He's driven at high speed down the hard shoulder of the motorway.

Banged up in Pentonville nick…

Then put on a plane to Sri Lanka.

*

Full-on display of state power.

13.

(*We let that sink in…*)

We burst like the clouds.

Pour forth.

From the church where the phone tree has brought us, for real this time.

Too late to stop the defeat. But.

Are we too late to save Viraj?

The man himself?

Not even the Sri Lankan government can kill Viraj with this light shining on him!

Can they?

Onwards.

We will stop Manchester.

Up Bonsall Street. Onto Oxford Road.

You shall not pass!

We swarm.

Onto Portland Street. Outside The Britannia we sit down.

We block the road.

We shall not be moved.

I see Mallard.

Serious. Professional. Letting this be.

Even he knows.

The eyes of the whole country are on this.

The whole world.

This is the moment.

*

Viraj is on a plane.

The cameras are there.

It's broadcast live on the news – all channels.

Can our beautiful man be kept safe by our rage?

Eventually Viraj escapes to Germany, where he lives to fight another day...

To his last day.

*

On that distant day, on the road, outside The Britannia,

We are unstoppable.

But stopped.

We're together.

But torn apart.

We're defeated.

But we link arms.

We sing.

We shout.

We are your enemy.

Till death.

We will never forget.

We will never forgive.

Viva Viraj Mendis!

May you rest in peace.

Our beautiful warrior.

(*End on the song.*)

EVE STEELE (original performer)

Eve Steele is a writer and actor who regularly performs in her own work, such as recent Radio 4 dramas *Reasons to Stay Alive* and *Torn,* stage plays *Work it Out* (HOME Theatre) and *Trial* (Monkeywood Theatre & Bolton Octagon) and short film *Transfiguration* (triptych of three short films) for Fallen Angels Dance Theatre.

Other acting credits include, Theatre: *The Political History of Smack & Crack* (Roundabout Edinburgh, Soho Theatre & national tour); *Life by the Throat* (national tour); *The Newspaper Boy* (53:two). TV includes: *Clink, Casualty, Scott & Bailey, Sleeping Lions, The Driver* and *Coronation Street.*

A Nick Hern Book

Ordinary Decent Criminal first published in Great Britain as a paperback original in 2025 by Nick Hern Books Limited, The Glasshouse, 49a Goldhawk Road, London W12 8QP

Ordinary Decent Criminal copyright © 2025 Ed Edwards

Sanctuary copyright © 2025 Ed Edwards

Ed Edwards has asserted his right to be identified as the author of these works

Cover image: Rebecca Need-Menear

Designed and typeset by Nick Hern Books, London
Printed in Great Britain by Mimeo Ltd, Huntingdon, Cambridgeshire PE29 6XX

A CIP catalogue record for this book is available from the British Library

ISBN 978 1 83904 482 3

CAUTION All rights whatsoever in this play are strictly reserved. Requests to reproduce the text in whole or in part should be addressed to the publisher. This book may not be used, in whole or in part, for the development or training of artificial intelligence technologies or systems.

Amateur Performing Rights Applications for performance, including readings and excerpts, by amateurs in the English language throughout the world should be addressed to the Performing Rights Manager, Nick Hern Books, The Glasshouse, 49a Goldhawk Road, London W12 8QP, *tel* +44 (0)20 8749 4953, *email* rights@nickhernbooks.co.uk, except as follows:

Australia: ORiGiN Theatrical, Level 1, 213 Clarence Street, Sydney NSW 2000, *tel* +61 (2) 8514 5201, *email* enquiries@originmusic.com.au, *web* www.origintheatrical.com.au

New Zealand: Play Bureau, 20 Rua Street, Mangapapa, Gisborne 4010, *tel* +64 21 258 3998, *email* info@playbureau.com

United States of America and Canada: Berlin Associates, see details below

Professional Performing Rights Applications for performance by professionals in any medium and in any language throughout the world (and amateur and stock performances in the United States of America and Canada) should be addressed to Berlin Associates, 7 Tyers Gate, London SE1 3HX, *fax* +44 (0)20 7632 5296, *email* agents@berlinassociates.com

No performance of any kind may be given unless a licence has been obtained. Applications should be made before rehearsals begin. Publication of these plays does not necessarily indicate their availability for performance.

www.nickhernbooks.co.uk/environmental-policy

Nick Hern Books' authorised representative in the EU is
Easy Access System Europe – Mustamäe tee 50, 10621 Tallinn, Estonia
email gpsr.requests@easproject.com